Since 2020

MW01240510

Written and Edited by Paul Doherty

Photography by the Stance Auto Media Team

This is a Monthly Car Magazine brought to you by Stance Auto and the car street scene, in this magazine you will find cars and real life stories from all over the world, groups and clubs that may be of interest to you, and some of the best Photography from some very talented photographers.

All these stories are from the actual owners of the cars, they will tell you about their life in the car street scene, what inspires them and some handy tips and advice for anyone thinking of buying the same car, all their Instagram tags and them of the photographers are here for you to follow, we also highlight the people in the trade who are supplying the parts helping to build these cars, we invite anyone and everyone with a hi-spec or modified car to submit their car and their story to feature in this magazine and also our online MAG, why don't you come along and join us in our Facebook group and get to know us and some of the owners, ask questions and submit your own car, you'll find we are all very friendly, this is a community for us all.

We also have Calendars, Hoodies, T-shirts, Magazines and Stickers available from our Store
Merchandise Store: stanceautomag.com and Etsy
To follow us, submit your car or join us check out our Links
Instagram:@stanceautomag
Facebook: @stanceautomag
Submit Your Car and Story: https://stanceauto.co.uk/submissions

Kevin Ricci
1991 Porsche 911 C4
Instagram: @U4EA4ME
Photographer: @jrice_visuals

I currently live in Houston, TX but am originally from Akron, OH. My day job is within the oil industry but my real passion is for all things car-related - I really enjoy detailing cars and do a lot of that in my spare time.

I also attend plenty of cars and coffee along with rally events and enjoy track days as often as I can. I'm a huge Porsche fan, but love to look at all types of builds and Houston is a great place to be for that!

Like most others, I got hooked on cars as a child with my Hot Wheels collections. I spent countless hours collecting and playing with them and I still collect them today.

As I grew up, my passion for cars didn't fade and I actually still have Car and Driver magazines from the '80s and '90s in my attic that I perused from time to time.

I went to some track days with my father when I was in high school and auto crossed my Integra LS in college but didn't really get into the show scene until I graduated and moved to Texas. I had a group of friends and we used to go to all the shows in and around Texas to compete and have fun.

I've had quite a few cars along the way and have modified them all. I prefer an OEM+ style and I think this car checks that box. The first car I truly modified was my 1998 Integra LS in college, I did all the basic bolt-ons and style changes.

I had that car for 7 years and ended up selling to buy a 2006 G35 that I went off the deep end with and after modifying it to the point of undriveability, I sold that and actually bought a 1976 Bronco.

It was a nice change to not have to dodge potholes and worry about road debris constantly! While I loved the Bronco, it was a constant headache and ultimately sold that one as well. The cars I have now are a 2009 911 Turbo and this 1991 911 C4 and both have been modified pretty heavily - I try not to completely detract from the original design but like to put my touches on anything I own.

I bought this car in 2017. I am fairly involved in the local PCA chapter and had always wanted an air-cooled car. The more time I spent judging them at local concourses and seeing them online, the more that I knew I wanted to own one. My turbo was my dream car (and still is) but this car has been an experience and I enjoy everything about it.

Originally I had wanted a colour that wasn't red, but I was unwilling to pay the premium that folks were asking for some of the more "skittles coloured" examples.

Ultimately I found this car, made a deal and purchased it sight unseen and had it shipped to me from Michigan. I already had the vision of what i wanted to do with the car and many of the parts were in order or in my garage before I had found the car so the modifications began almost immediately.

This car is just plain fun. There are faster cars, but this one brings a smile to my face. You can drive it fast or slow and the same feeling persists. While the turbo is fun at speed, this car is fun at 20 mph. Listening to the air-cooled engine sing is great and the smell and sounds that this car delivers are exactly what driving a 911 should be.

The car always gets looks, waves and thumbs up which always makes you feel good. I love hearing people's stories when I stop to get gas. I usually have someone stop by to ask about the car, no-one believes me when I tell them it is a 91 and is 30 years old! I love seeing people interact with the car as it reminds me of the way I felt when I was young. I love letting others sit in the car for pictures, or just to get a feel of what an old 911 is like... it's perfect!

STANCEAUTOMAG JEREMY RICE

STANCEAUTOMAG JEREMY RICE

Advice/Tip

My advice for anyone considering buying one of these air-cooled cars is two-fold. First, make sure you really want one - many people think they want one because they hear others talk about them. They are not for everyone especially at the inflated values they have gotten to nowadays.

You can buy a lot of really great cars that will perform better and be more reliable for the money - if that is a concern, you may want to look elsewhere. Also, be prepared for repairs - these cars were neglected for years before they sky rocketed in value, so finding a good example is hard and even those will likely need some TLC and money to keep running reliably. That being said, you will have a lot of fun in one and they will hold their value well if that is a concern for you.

Mod Tips

My only advice for modifying this car is to do what you want, don't listen to others. People will always have comments, especially in the Porsche world - there are purists and there are those that like to tweak and modify and there is plenty of room for both in the world. Find a style or path you like and go for it!

I think what makes this car unique is the wheels. People always tell me how much they like the wheels as they are very similar to the phone dials found on the 924/944. Once you get past the wheels, the next comment is "wow that is really low, do you drive at that height?" and the answer is yes it is low and yes I do drive at that height. It can be a challenge but the car still handles pretty well with the big wheels and low stance. Lastly, the houndstooth interior is always a big hit with people when they see the car.

Shout Outs

I have had a lot of help getting the car to this point and am super appreciative of the awesome local shops we have available to us.

A few local shops who have always helped and done an excellent job are:

Modern Air cooled - @modernaircooled has always gone above and beyond to keep the car running in tip-top shape.

Sublime Heights - @sublimeheights did the interior work and couldn't be more pleased!

Sals Auto Sport - @salsautosport did the paintwork and stereo install and always keeps the alignment dialled in!

STANCEAUTOMAG JEREMY RICE

Interior:
- Full custom houndstooth interior
- Alpine Bluetooth radio
- Rennline pedals and floorboard
- Lloyd mats
- Porsche RS steering wheel
- Commune DIY custom shift knob
- Swine11 shifter reboot

Engine/Transmission:
- G Pipe
- Steve Wong Chip
- Patrick Motorsports LWFW
- FD Motorsports goldenrod
- FD Motorsports Transmission Mount
- FD Motorsports short shifter
- Rennline motor mounts

Exterior:
- RUF front lip
- Porsche RS air ducts
- Custom tinted clear corners
- LED's
- 9eleven headlights
- Aero mirrors
- Custom Porsche hood badge

Future Plans

I'd like to add some bucket seats and start sprucing up the engine bay with some tweaks in the future but am happy with how she sits at the moment so not in any rush.

The car scene has been good to me. Most of the friends I have made in Texas, I've met through the car scene whether at shows or gatherings etc. I moved here in 2009 and I didn't know anyone, so for me, cars were a way of meeting and ultimately connecting with people and making lifelong friends as a result, so I am extremely grateful for that.

My dream car is the 2009 911 Turbo I own, but if money was no object and I could have any car I wanted - you'd see me in an F40 or a Mclaren F1 GTR!

Wheels:
- Rotiform 18" STR
Suspension:
- Rotiform/H&R Deep Coilovers

STANCEAUTOMAG JEREMY RICE

Dan P.
2007 Porsche Cayman S

Instagram: @Bagged_Cayman
Photographer: @Jrice_visuals - @cr2hannah

I am a native Texan who runs a small Data/IT firm in Houston that loves working on my crazy builds in my free time and chilling with my dogs.

I have always loved cars, in high school, I used to get an Import Tuner on the way home from school and dream about building my own car. My parents on the other hand were not car people and thought buying a magazine was a waste of money, but they did let me go to San Jacinto for Automotive school after I graduated.

I got in trouble many times with my parents for making modifications to my vehicles without their approval.

This is the first Porsche I have ever owned and the first car that I have done a widebody on, I have built other cars before but mostly only performance work and never show car material.

I was looking for a new daily and had test drove some 911s but they were always out of my price range. I then test drove a friend's Cayman S and that was when I knew I wanted one. Little did I know that one week after I bought it I would have been involved in a hit and run that damaged the entire passenger side. From then on it became a project car.

The feeling is surreal, I had always dreamed of owning an actual car you would see in conventions, magazines and VIP line ups at car shows, to walk into my garage every day and see it sitting there still makes me smile.

The Porsche Tax is Real!!! Every after market part for this car is expensive, but on the other hand, very well made and always worth the money you spend.

Be ready for the Porsche Purists to hate any crazy modification you do to it. There are very few Pandem Widebody Caymans in the US, with me being 1 of only 2 in all of Texas. On top of that, I hand made my splitters and diffusers so there are non exactly like mine.

After the car was hit, I ordered the kit from Japan and that took 3-4 months to arrive, after that it went to a body shop that installed and painted it the factory colour of Carrera white. After I got the car back I did the rest of the build myself ie. suspension, exhaust, wheels, air ride.

Future Plans
My next couple of major mods are a full chassis mount wing, race seats and full interior upholstery.

I am a member of Beyond City Limits - A growing group of fellow car enthusiasts whose main focus is making new connections with owners and not just their rides. The car scene here has been amazing, their support of the build is what keeps me motivated to push the limits of my creativity. I am grateful that I have made so many new and amazing friends over the last couple of months of like-minded people who have a love for cars.

BAG RIDERS ◆ HANNAH DURASO

BAG RIDERS HANNAH DURASO

Spec List

Engine
EVOMSit Intelligent ECU Tune
Fabspeed Long Tube Race Headers
Fabspeed Super cup Race Exhaust System
B&M Short Shifter

Exterior
Pandem V2 Widebody
Underglow.us 6 Row 480w Color Chase Underglow

Interior
HIP Design Clear Engine Cover

Wheels
Forgestar F14
Front 19x10 (-12 Offset) - Cooper Zeon RS3-G1 255/35
Rear 19x12 (-50 Offset) - Cooper Zeon RS3-G1 305/30

Suspension and Brakes
Yellow Speed Racing Dynamic Pro Air Struts
R1 Concepts - R1 Carbon Driller Rotors & Performance
Sport Pads

Austin Tague
2019 EcoBoost Mustang

Instagram: @chaotic_s550
Photographer: @merrick_media

I am 24 years old and currently work in the oil fields and have been doing that for 5 years now.

I have been into cars for as long as I can remember. Cars and video games have always been my passion, when I'm not at work, I'm either doing something to my car or streaming on Twitch.

The Mustang is the first car I ever purchased which was a huge accomplishment for me. Especially since I have owned somewhere around 15 cars since I was 18.

I am currently a part of the Chaotic Society and have been for about a year and a half now. They are an amazing group of people I would even go as far as saying they are more of a family than a group or club.

I can truly say that the car scene has changed my life, most of my closest friends are more like family now, I have met because of the car scene. Whether it be from a car meet, car show or even just selling or buying car parts, I've met incredible people because of it.

My dad was the one who got me into cars at a very young age, he was a circle track racer.

He drove circle track dirt racing for most of my childhood which is what really kicked off my passion for cars.

He would take me to the racetrack every weekend and once a year he would take me to a car show in Corpus Christi called Heat Wave which opened my eyes to modified cars other than race cars.

The mustang is far from my first car but is my first domestic vehicle. I have always loved imports, I have owned 1 of my dream cars which was an R32 Nissan Skyline that I imported from Japan. Most of my other vehicles ranged from Nissan 240s to BMW's but no matter what car I owned it had to have a turbo which is what led me in the direction of buying the eco boost.

To be truthful I never thought I would own a mustang but a good friend of mine let me drive him and after I did I knew I had to buy one. The car is so comfortable and a perfect mixture of daily driver and track car all in one. The eco boost platform is perfect for people that are into imports but what to give a go at owning and modifying a domestic vehicle.

Owning this car has been a very unique feeling because of the modifications I have done to the car. It's not easy to drive anywhere unnoticed. All of the attention I get ranges from good and bad because like most builds, you can never please everyone. An example of the good is how awesome it is seeing kids get excited when I drive by them because it reminds me of the excitement I got when seeing a modified car when I was their age.

Even though there are a lot of "stanced" s550 Mustangs being done I personally think everyone's build has their own unique parts. Like my car having the 4" blast pipes and a Cobra R hood and GT350 front bumper which is something you don't normally see on eco boost lets my car stand out from others.

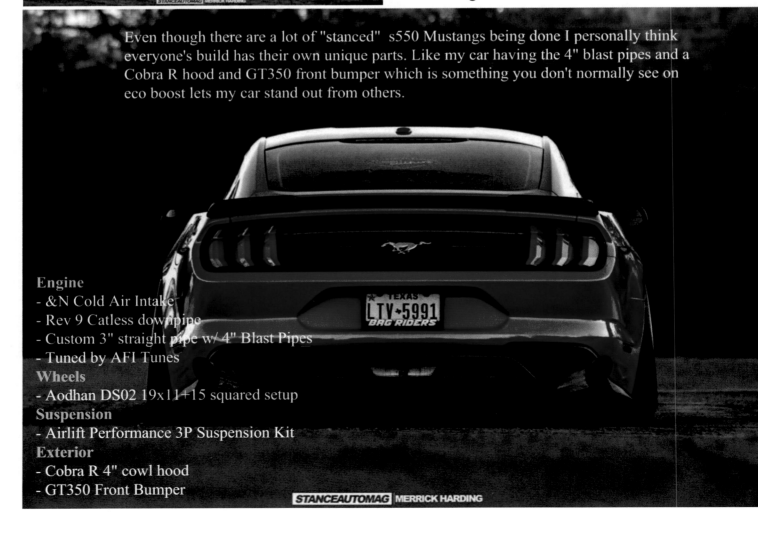

Engine
- &N Cold Air Intake
- Rev 9 Catless downpipe
- Custom 3" straight pipe w/ 4" Blast Pipes
- Tuned by AFI Tunes

Wheels
- Aodhan DS02 19x11+15 squared setup

Suspension
- Airlift Performance 3P Suspension Kit

Exterior
- Cobra R 4" cowl hood
- GT350 Front Bumper

Hopefully, in the near future, I would like to go full e85 and big turbo on the car to make as much power as possible and test the limits of the 2.3L EcoBoost motor.

As for exterior mods, I would like to do so in the future. I want to keep it simple for now. I want to add a GT350R track pack spoiler, some kind of aggressive rear diffuser and a custom-built set of GMR 3pc wheels. Possibly once the car is paid off and I have something new I might decide to do a full wide-body on the car but that won't be for a good while.

Most of the work I have done on my own but I've always had coilovers on all of my cars so when it came to installing bags I had to call in for some help. A good friend of mine has his own company selling and installing suspension parts and wheels so he was able to help me knock out the install pretty quickly on the car.

My number 1 dream car is a 1998 Toyota Mk4 Supra imported from Japan. Ever since I saw the supra in the original Fast and Furious I knew I had to own one at some point in my life.

Diego Navarro
2015 Ford Mustang
50-year edition

Instagram: @diegocertified - @theredmus
Twitter: @adndiegonavarro
Youtube: Diego Certified

I am originally from Colombia but I have lived in Miami Florida for 7 years. I have always liked cars, trucks, and motorcycles.

I love the speed and adrenaline of the drag strips and especially the car audio world, which I have experienced for 22 years designing and manufacturing some of the most dazzling and powerful demonstration vehicles that have had a huge impact around the world.

It all started when as a child when I first got into a car that had the lows and felt the intense vibration of the bass. I was shocked through all my body and that adrenaline was my greatest inspiration to dedicate my whole life to car audio.

Now I celebrate 22 years of a career full of sustained successes with DS18 which is experiencing amazing growth for the last consecutive 7 years that it was formed.

It has positioned itself as a leading company in the American car audio market, and as a competitor I have been awarded 20 times as champion in 12 different categories.

My beginnings in the world of "custom" cars began with my first car, a 79' Renault which I modified all the doors to open up as a butterfly. I brushed the handles and they opened up with a remote control, I used a double-tone paint with frost and it attracted a lot of attention wherever it was. I liked that a lot because I felt that it is a way of expression on wheels and step-up from the others.

So that was 20 years ago! and over time I improved and got all kinds of vehicles like a 95' Ford bronco filled with crazy powerful audio speakers, a 2001 Ford excursion with 160 DB's of bass pressure, a 2005 Jetta turbo, a full customized 2011 Mazda 3, a C5 corvette… BUT!! in 2015, Ford came out with its new generation of Mustangs and was struck with the modern and aggressive lines of the authentic American muscle car that characterizes it.

And after that it became my goal to achieve and to have that icon at the door of my house. It was not easy due to my economic situation at that time to be able to afford it, so I had to plan "how to" achieve that goal.

So, I began to modify and sell the cars that I was using as my daily to get a profit and go up in value every time.

I started to buy cheap cars and modify them aesthetically, such as   It is the cleanest thing I could have found and what I could afford at the time, it only had one "but" it had the 2.3-liter EcoBoost engine!

It's not a big deal and it didn't seem bad to me at the time because what I was interested in is how the car looks but not how fast it could go, and it was running well enough and it saved me gas! So, I started little by little to make both aesthetic and performance modifications,

I continued until one day I could gather enough to finally buy my favourite car! and by luck of fate I found this 2015 ford mustang 50 year edition in very pristine condition with very low mileage for 20K!

It is the cleanest thing I could have found and what I could afford at the time, it only had one "but" it had the 2.3-liter EcoBoost engine!

It's not a big deal and it didn't seem bad to me at the time because what I was interested in is how the car looks but not how fast it could go, and it was running well enough and it saved me gas! So, I started little by little to make both aesthetic and performance modifications,

First I started with dropping the car 2 inches using a lowering springs kit from Eibach and 20" wheels staggered from Concave wheels, then the audio system, which started with 3 10-inch subwoofer and 1000W in total all DS18 of course!

In terms of performance, I started with the cold air intake filter and the turbo blow-off valve, so that was it for a while… until one day my boss told me that we had to use something new for our booth at SEMA in Las Vegas Nevada, and use this car as a DS18 Demo Vehicle for "Tuners" car shows and events around the country.

So that changed everything in the history of this car and started a full process of modifications bumper to bumper on it! With the help of KK Customs Corp, Mishimoto, Glassskinz, Lighting Trendz, Whistler group, True Spikes Lug nuts, Baer Brakes, Vertini Wheels, Pro Clip USA and DS18 as sponsors of this build.

This became a dream come true to have my own car displayed in the world famous and world biggest event of the car industry the SEMA Show. But this does not end there, after having Debuted at SEMA and CES in Las Vegas, the car returned to Miami and a short time later the engine broke down, a serious fault in the turbo caused oil to flow into the cylinders, bending the connecting rods and causing a considerable damage to the engine, cylinders, bending the connecting rods and causing a considerable damage to the engine, it made me think about my next project with this car!

Making the first "Swap" engine from an Eco-Boost to a third generation of Coyote V8 with a 10-speed transmission in a 2015 mustang!

Why did I do it? First of all, all my friends were bullying me for having a 4-cylinder engine on an "American muscle car". Second, I always liked the sound of a V8 and finally it is something that no one had recorded on YouTube or posted on the internet before, so I wanted to be the first to do it and I did it!

In addition to putting a new MY 2020 engine with its transmission, all the bolt-ons were put like long header cat-less with 3-inch Cat-back, Cold Air Intake, Tuned ECU, Digital Cluster, among other things making this, "one of a kind" which is my greatest pride!

zoey engle
2009 Nissan 370Z

Instagram: @zoeyengle
Photographer: @samuel.originals

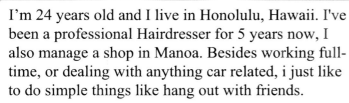

I'm 24 years old and I live in Honolulu, Hawaii. I've been a professional Hairdresser for 5 years now, I also manage a shop in Manoa. Besides working full-time, or dealing with anything car related, i just like to do simple things like hang out with friends.

When I was younger my dad used to have a 2005 bright yellow mustang and everyday we would be cleaning it, taking hours and hours. I wasn't too interested at first but after a while I would go down stairs to watch and just to hang out.

I would see the love and passion he had for it in his eyes and the way he did everything with it, it inspired me to learn or understand why he feels this way.

My dad had a good heart but he was very focused on what he did or wanted mostly so learning things from him was very difficult.

The only thing he would let me do was hold the flashlight and tell me to watch, it killed my motivation to learn anything about cars. Every time he would ask me for my opinion for this part or what sticker or what color, and he would always pick the answer I didn't say.

I just wanted to be like him and to be useful. So one day we got into a small argument and I told him one day I'll have the car that I want, I'll learn on my own and work hard to put my own money towards it so I won't need your opinion.

This is my first car, I got it when I was 22 years old. As every teenager who has their license wants a car right away or get a new one I had to wait.

I ended up getting my license at 17 years old, I was a senior in high school and at the same time my parents got a divorce. I didn't get a car for my birthday or as a gift but instead I got a job.

I remember what I said when I was younger and I wasn't gonna lose focus. My mom would let me use her car if i needed too so i never really needed one of my own nor did we have the money for it.

It was my dad's favourite car and whenever he got a chance to look at one he would take it.

That's all he would ever talk about. He wasn't the safest driver or nicest so he had a ticket after ticket. It was getting so bad to the point where my mom hated the car, turns out all the money he put toward it was my mom's money.

It was like bad luck to her, so I went looking in JDM. Saw a bunch of different builds and started looking up parts and trying to piece together what would suit me best.

From 17 to 20 I was working full time thinking about my career and what I should do so in 2016 I went to a Barber school and graduated a year later in 2017.

I started as a receptionist in 2015 and within 4 years I became the manager. Knowing that i finally had something that I was gonna stick with for a long time made me feel extremely confident that I could get my own car.

I bought my car in April, 2018 and that's when everything started. The only sports car that I was ever around were mustangs.

I ended up with my 370z and a vision so I got to work. My love for this car has no words, I'm just proud to own it and have my vision come to life. When I got it back from paint was the day I turned heads. It was the best day of my life. I'm glad it makes people happy and it's the best feeling when people talk to me about it or ask questions.

Especially when girls come up to me to ask questions or even just to admire it because the car scene is dominated by men and I want them to know that they can do it too just gotta find the right people to help you. I built my car mostly for me, it was a goal that I knew I could accomplish.

Spec List

Exterior:
- Custom paint @waifuworks
- Custom headlights @riesphotography
- Underglow @ledglow
- Spoiler @battleaero
- Aimgain body kit
- Clear PPF @autotrimhawaii

Interior:
- Custom cherry blossom headliner
- Quick release steering wheel @getnrg
- Interior lights @ledglow
- Custom shifter @mr__grip

Wheels:
- Work emotions (daily)
- 3-piece Sevenk nika (show)
- Akebono big brakes kit

Suspension:
- Airlift performance

VQINC @vqinchawaii

Vqinc gave me the chance and opportunity to build this car my way, they accepted me with open arms and believed in me every step of the way.

They care about all the members and try to help with anything they can. They teach me everything about this car and how things work. Very grateful to be a part of this club.

I can only do simple things but with my great friends they teach me and help me better understand my Z and I'm forever grateful.

Mike Tengasantos @miketenga
Justin Rapozo @tgstig808
Zac Hioki @zachioki & @waifuworks
VQINC @vqinchawaii
Tokyo auto @tokyoauto
Chad Ries @riesphotography
RoninDivision @ronindivision
Alan tran @alannn.trannn
Keiko Soohoo @keikrrrs
Revision Audio @revisionaudio_samson

Cassandra Leal
2018 Honda Civic Sport FK7

Instagram: @lolfk7
Photographer: @buckys_photography

I'm 25 years old and I'm from Dinuba, CA. I drive a 2018 Honda Civic Sport Hatchback. It has a 1.5-litre turbocharged engine with a 6-Speed manual transmission. I'm currently a bartender/server at Ridgecreek Golf Course.

I hope to one day become an Automotive Technician. I spend most of my days at work but outside of that, I love to hang out with my friends and cousins. I love to go to Burnyard Bash, Formula Drift and Car Shows/Meets.

I was always into cars but I definitely have to give credit to my cousins, Roberto, Jacob & Sergio. They've had the biggest influence on me.

They're the ones that started taking me to car meets and car shows where I was able to fully get into the car scene. Being a girl, I never really knew anybody that was into cars so it was hard for me to know where to even start. They've taught me so much.

My first car was a 2004 Volkswagen Golf. It wasn't very reliable and lasted me maybe a couple of years. I didn't get the chance to do any kind of modifications because it was always in the mechanics. After I got rid of it, I didn't have a car for a few years. I finally bought my Civic and knew right away that I wanted to mod it.

This car is the first-ever car that I bought on my own. The reason I picked it is because I wanted something reliable. At the time of purchase, my family really needed a car to transport my little sister to almost daily hospital visits.

Aside from needing something reliable for my family, I wanted something cute that was my style for myself. I loved everything about it when I first saw it. It was super cute and sporty and totally me! I didn't even test drive it! I saw it and got started on paperwork right away. I just knew it was the one.

It's so much fun both driving and owning this car. I absolutely love my car. I take pictures of it every day and just smile when I see it parked. My favourite thing about it is the daily props and thumbs up I get when I'm just driving around. I put a lot into my car, not for everyone to love it, but for myself. It's still really nice to get some positive feedback from people. It might sound silly but my car brings me so much happiness!

Advice/Tips
My only advice would be to take your time and have fun with it. Don't rush it and don't take the easy way out. Be good to your car and it will be good to you!

What makes it Unique?
So many people have these cars so it's hard to build one that doesn't look like someone else's. I'd have to say what makes my car unique is the glittery/sparkly theme I have going on. Mostly my glittery roof. It's definitely a neck breaker and it hasn't been done before on my type of car. People are always asking questions about it and taking pictures.

My dream car is a Nissan 240SX. I actually owned one for a short amount of time but had to get rid of it. It's the first car I fell in love with when I was first getting into cars. I hope that when I get one again I can build it and become a drift queen!

STANCEAUTOMAG BUCKY HOHOLIK

There's been a lot of people that have helped make my car what it is today and I'm so beyond grateful. I've had most of the help from my fiancé, cousins and tons of friends.

I've helped with a few things but I mostly try to watch and learn. I'm fortunate to have great friends and family that take the time to not only help me install things but help me learn as well.

Future Plans

I'm definitely hoping to get some new wheels soon. I've had the same setup for some time now and I really want to change things up a little bit. I also want to get another seat for my passenger side.

I don't have very many future plans because I'm not in a rush to build my car. I'm going to have this car for as long as I possibly can. These things take a lot of time, so I just try to have fun with them and give myself time to think about my next mod.

Spec List

Interior:
- NRG Quick Release Steering Wheel,
- NRG Prisma Racing Seat,
- NRG Harness,
- Cipher Auto Harness Bar with Custom Paint,
- DC Sports Weighted Shift Knob

Engine:
- PRL Cobra Cold Air Intake,
- KTuner V1.2, Muffler/Resonator Delete

Exterior:
- ABS Dynamics Type R Wing,
- Custom Painted Roof

Wheels and Suspension
- ESR SR13
- BC Racing Coilovers

Groups/Clubs

I am currently a Prospect Member for Team NVUS. My chapter is the Origin Chapter (@nvus_origin). I joined a couple of months ago after not being a part of a car group or club for over a year. I saw that they give back to the community a lot and I knew that I needed to be a part of the team. I reached out and they welcomed me with open arms. They're a solid team and they're definitely family to me.

What I love most about the car scene are all the friendships that come out of it. You meet so many people and build the most solid friendships ever. If you ever need help with something or you're feeling bored and just want to meet up at a target parking lot, someone is just a call or text away! Most of the people you meet become family. Growing up, I never had a lot of friends and never really felt included in anything. I can definitely say that I found myself and found where I fit in with the car scene.

José Velázquez
2016 RWD Lexus Is200t F-Sport

Instagram: @El_Casper09
Instagram: @Black_Pearls716
Photographer: @fireblazinmedia

My name is Jose Velazquez, I am 21 years old and currently live in Buffalo NY but born and raised in Puerto Rico. I just got done with my military contract so now I do construction Full time. I've been into cars since possibly starting to walk.

Everyone here in buffalo knows that if there's anything car-related they'll get there and you'll see my car upfront, I feel like it's just an amazing feeling when you can stand out and not look like common traffic.

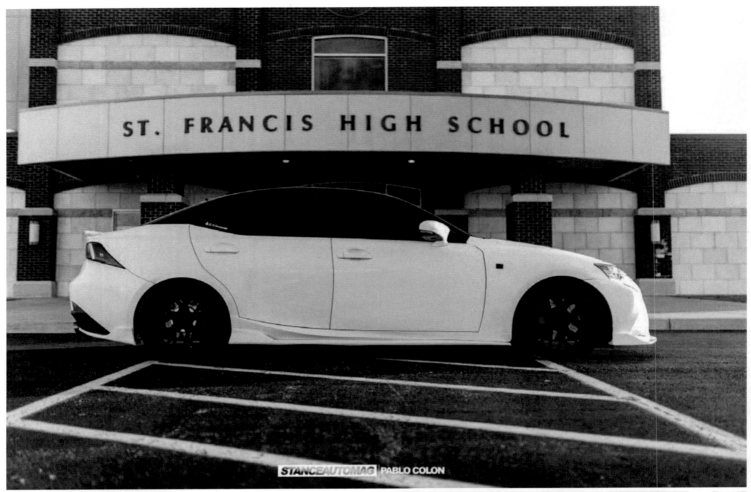

The way my passion for cars started was by my parents playing the F&F movies for me over and over, then buying me a PS1 with Gran Turismo, it went from that to midnight club, and so on.

My first car was a 2000 Honda Civic Ex Coupe and that right there taught me the real value of being into cars, not worrying how you're dressed when something breaks you get down under the car and fix it, how all builds could be appreciated and how all of us have different taste but as long as you're comfortable and love your personal vehicle and it puts a smile on your face when you turn around you're doing it right.

Another thing I learned is that in the Car scene you'll meet people that start as friends and end up being family when we're all staying up late trying to fix a car figure out a problem or even just the joy of riding together as a group breaking necks everywhere we go.

Now I did a little upgrade and got myself a RWD 2016 Lexus is200t F-Sport. This car right here is my prized possession, my ongoing project even though it's hard to find more things to do there's never enough.

Why A Lexus you ask, well the reason I decided to go with this car was that I normally didn't see it around where I'm always at in like the west side of buffalo, etc I only used to see it in the suburbs so it was a luxury car I thought I could make sporty and what makes it unique well I have a whole custom interior sound system that I could take out and use it as a huge boom box as well.

Spec List
Performance:

- Injen Intake with an K&N Air filter
- Pedal Commander throttle body response booster
- Jb4 Bluetooth Kit
- PPE DownPipe catless
- Remark Axle-back Exhaust
- Resonator delete
- Drilled & slotted rotors
- Ksport Coilovers

Extras:
- Alpine (Extra radio)
- Eight PRV 8" mid bass speakers
- 7 PRV Drivers
- Solid Audio equalizer for the speakers
- Massive audio equalizer for the drivers
- Tímpano, cross over
- 2 12" Power acoustic Subwoofers in a ported box
- Lanzar vector amp for the subwoofers
- Tarramps amp for the speakers
- Planet audio amp for the drivers
Everything is powered by one extra battery including the cars

Looks:

- JM Auto Racing front lip
- JM Auto Racing side skirts
- JM Auto racing rear bumper corner apron Spats
- LS009 Aodhan 20x9 +30 Black
- Ninte rear spoiler
- Avs rain guards
- Tinted 20% all around including windshield
- Roof and a bit of the rear 1/4 panel Wrapped gloss black and ceramic coated
- Full chrome delete with a custom F Sport emblem
Slightly rolled Fenders

Future plans
- MV tuning hood
- Full Wrap
- Air suspension
And possibly a couple of secret components for the engine so I can make more power

Andy Kim
2014 Hyundai Veloster Turbo

Instagram: @vt_andy
Photographer: @buckys_photography

I was born in Los Angeles California and joined the Navy right out of high school where I've been stationed in Jacksonville, FL, Patuxent River, MD, and now Lemoore, CA.

What got me into cars you ask so I'm from LA where the import scene has been huge since the beginning. Grew up loving the older model Honda's with CWEST Kits and the crazy neons. Even had those shirts hung on my wall with the Honda's if you know you know. My first car was a 1994 Acura Integra LS which I didn't do much of since I was still in high school with no job, just modding the car of my lunch money. But after joining the Navy I purchased a 1997 Acura Integra RS which had a JDM front end with a B18C1 motor swap.

From there I went a totally different route and wanted something I figured no one would like which was a 2009 Honda Fit Sport built to look clean for its tiny little 1.5L engine. Sold that and moved onto my current 2014 Hyundai Veloster Turbo.

Why this Car?

I got this car because I have a tendency to purchase unique cars and hatchbacks. I like to challenge myself and get cars no one would think of modifying and make them look clean. The Veloster as some of you know has 3 doors. Yes, 3 doors! 1 driver / 1 passenger / 1 rear passenger. That caught my eye and it was a turbo! who knew it would be so fun!

The way this car looks makes me extremely happy. I end up always looking back at it after parking and to be able to show off my hard work at local shows and big shows. I can tell people appreciate the attention to detail on small things and It gives me the motivation to continue modding. When you drive by or park at a show the one kid that says "Look dad look at that car!!" makes it all worth it.

Advice/Tips

2 tips I can give about this car is it's fun to mod but very limited to what you can do. One source from great parts are scgarageworks.com they are based in Southern California and is the only place you can get good quality products for the Veloster and Greg the owner is amazing with customer service.

Another tip is if you get this car make sure you use OEM oil filters like any car, there have been instances with other Veloster owners where non-OEM filters would leak oil or not perform well. Modifying tips I would give is to avoid modifying the headlights. The headlights are so big and awkward that it's a pain to take apart and modify.

What makes it Unique?

I think what makes my car so unique is the orange colour and the wide fender flares. I know when people see a stock Veloster vs. my car they can't believe how much I've done.

Groups/Clubs

I am part of @NvUS. We all motivate each other to make our builds better. NvUS is a worldwide club that wants to be known for being dignified, respectful, and community-oriented. NvUS motto,
"We Support Those Who Support Us."
Being a part of NvUS is like having a second family. We always help each other in any way possible and always have a great time together even if it's just having a small BBQ.

If I end up in a bad situation I can always count on one of my fellow members to help me and pick me up.

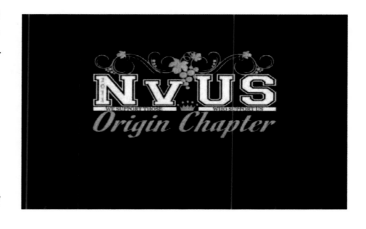

Engine:

- 845 Motorsports Front Mount Intercooler w/ Synapse DV
- HKS M45XL Spark Plugs
- Tork Motorsports Stage 1 Tune
- Tork Motorsports Catless Downpipe
- 6th Element Engineering Stainless Steel Fuel Line
- ADD W1 Catch Can x2
- Injen Short Ram Intake
- Muffler Delete
- Custom Dipstick
- Custom painted Engine Cowling

Interior:

- BRAUM Venom Series Sport Seats, Black Fabric, Red Stitches
- BRAUM 5pt Harness
- Diamond Stitched Floor Mats
- 6" Katana shifter
- So cal garage works D-Cut Steering Wheel
- Custom painted trim

Suspension:

- AIRTEKK Air suspension with ACCUAIR E-Level Management
- UNIQ Front Strut Bar
- Turbo socks Rigid Collars
- Pierce Motorsports Front Cross member 4point Support Brace
- Pierce Motorsports Rear Torsion Bar
- Pierce Motorsports Half Cage
- Pierce Motorsports Tubular Cross member

Most of the modifications I have done myself except the install of the air suspension, custom front lip, tail lights and headlights. One tip I can give about doing fender flares or widebody is to take it extremely slow and make sure you measure twice and cut once.

Future Plans

I want to do a wire tuck from the engine bay and run hard lines for the air suspension. But eventually, I want to move onto a Tesla Model 3 and modify that.

Dream Car

My dream car is a 1995 Acura NSX. The funny thing is my friend has an NSX and I'm too tall to fit in it but I would find a way if I can purchase that car.

Exterior:

- So Cal Garage works Full Mesh Grill with ABS Honey Comb
- STI lip
- MACTEC Design Splitter
- Clinched 7mm fender flares
- Work CR2P 18x11 +15
- Federal 55RSR 245/35
- Rally Armour mud flaps
- Custom made side skirt extension
- Weathertech window deflectors
- RSW GT Wing
- AEROWOLF End plates
- AEROWOLF Canards
- Custom painted headlights
- Exiled Rear Reflector Micom LED Modules Ver.2
- ILLUMAESTHETIC Tail lights
- Cappelletti design Color Chasing Kit RGBW Eye line/Halos
- The retro fit source 4000k HID kit
- The Retro fit Source 4000k Fog Light HID kit
- EVO VIII Vortex diffuser
- Sickspeed Dual Horns
- EGR Bug Shield
- Rola Roof Rack
- Cargo Box

Instagram: @xxaustd_wrx
Photographer: @Bucky_photography

Bill Sing
2013 Subaru Wrx Hatch

STANCEAUTOMAG BUCKY HOHOLIK

So I'm from Fresno California my hobby other than cars is being a musician for my church, going fishing, videography and photography as well.

What got me into cars was the "Fast and the Furious" sequel. I was more interested in the chill laid back and being a one-car family in the movie, not the racing lol why I got the hatch was because of "Brian" (Paul Walker) Midnight Club was another that really got me into cars especially when you can mod the cars lol So I've been a car enthusiast most of my life. A few years ago I built a page for our local car enthusiasts and it's been amazing!!

We have meets every Thursdays now (thirsty Thursdays) we all would come out and enjoy each other's ride while supporting the local Boba Shops.

My first big car event I went to was in Long Beach for WekFest and boy I had a fun time there!! So many quality builds there!! I believe without God, my family, friends and CARS I would go crazy!

My first car after graduation was the Honda Civic it was an automatic which I don't mind since it's taking me to college... l later then I got a Mitsubishi Lancer then trade that in for a 2013 Subaru wrx hatch which was always my dream of owning one I would pass by this hatch every morning going to work so after the 4th day of passing it I decided to purchase it.

STANCEAUTOMAG BUCKY HOHOLIK

It's been a dream for me to own a Subaru hatchback.

Like I said earlier it was because of Paul Walker's hatch that has inspired me to get one at first, it was just the visors on the doors, you know once you do one thing it leads to another and before you know it—you're broke lol if you're curious this is the first Manual car I've ever driven, thanks to my brother in law for teaching me.

Feels great now that I can call this my car!! Finally got it all paid off. I've always been a fan of Subaru starting with the Hawkeye but I love the stink eye which is my 2013 wrx hatch version of the headlights lol if you don't know when people say "Hawkeyes" "blob eyes" or "stink eye" then you shouldn't own a Subaru lol the 2015+ didn't have a name.

Advice/Tips

If you're thinking of buying a Subaru or with any car be sure to do the basic maintenance to keep your car running smoothly and longevity. Everything takes time. Set a goal to accomplish and not rush. Get authentic products that don't cheap your way out just because of funds but save your money.

Just When you're modding your car it's okay to ask questions from friends or get ideas but at the end of the day, you're making it yours because you own it so it's up to you to make any drastic decisions, because you should be building your car for yourself not the clout.

Groups/Clubs

I made Cencal automotive meet for the locals here in central California so we can get together and hang out and if there was anyone or anything happening we would find it in one place.

I'm not in any team but I'm so glad to have met a lot of car buddies due to the same passion. Sometimes we would go on a cruise or just go up to the mountains just to take photos of our cars. Anyone can add me on my Instagram page as well.

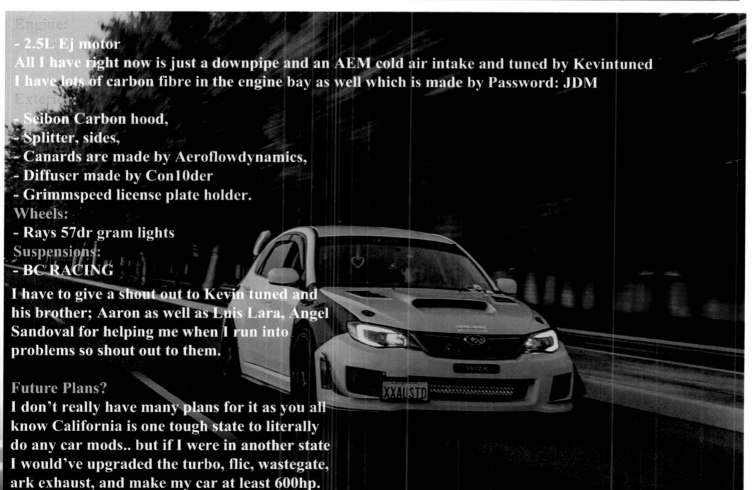

Engine:
- 2.5L Ej motor
All I have right now is just a downpipe and an AEM cold air intake and tuned by Kevintuned
I have lots of carbon fibre in the engine bay as well which is made by Password: JDM
Exterior:
- Seibon Carbon hood,
- Splitter, sides,
- Canards are made by Aeroflowdynamics,
- Diffuser made by Con10der
- Grimmspeed license plate holder.
Wheels:
- Rays 57dr gram lights
Suspensions:
- BC RACING

I have to give a shout out to Kevin tuned and his brother; Aaron as well as Luis Lara, Angel Sandoval for helping me when I run into problems so shout out to them.

Future Plans?
I don't really have many plans for it as you all know California is one tough state to literally do any car mods.. but if I were in another state I would've upgraded the turbo, flic, wastegate, ark exhaust, and make my car at least 600hp.

Matt Rollo
2017 Subaru WRX

Instagram: @lyfonair
Photographer: @fireblazinmedia

By the time I drove this car off the lot I already had new white Sparco wheels and the Subaru OEM under spoiler kit sitting in my room.

At the time, I knew that was all I was ever going to do to the car. That lasted a whole week before I found Subispeed.com and saw all the insane ways you can mod these cars.

You see, I've always wanted a cool JDM car ever since my first car. That was a 1993 Nissan 240SX. This was before it became the iconic JDM drift car that it is now, so I didn't really know what I had at the time other than a really cool looking car.

To this day I still geek out whenever I see a 240SX at a car show.

This build has been a work in progress ever since I bought it and I don't think it'll ever be "done." I get a lot of the motivation to keep this build going from my friends.

Some of my closest friends have some pretty insane builds. And when you see them pushing their build to see how far they can take it, it makes you want to do the same thing.

Mod list

Exterior mods
- Seibon Carbon Fiber front lip
- Enforced Aero front splitter
- SubiSpeed V2 Redline sequential LED headlights
- Seibon CW Style Carbon Fiber hood
- Wedssport SA-77R wheels wrapped in Achilles ATR Sport 2 tires
- Carbon fibre side mirror and door handle covers
- JDMuscle Tanso vented carbon fibre fenders
- Carbon fibre fender emblems
- Seibon GT-Style carbon fibre wing
- APR carbon fibre license plate backing
- ST-Style carbon fibre trunk trim
- Subaru OEM STI style side skirts and rear diffuser
- Inozetek Dandelion Yellow car wrap with a gloss black roof wrap
- JDMuscle Tanso Carbon Fiber grill
- Airlift suspension with Airlift 3S management

Interior mods
- JDMuscle Custom Carbon Fiber steering wheel
- Shift solutions Co weighted shift knob
- Carbon fibre shift trim and cup holders
- Custom ebrake boot and shift boot
- Custom yellow floor liner by Lux Auto Mat
- Custom airlift trunk setup
- Braum Racing White Elite-X Racing Seats
- Engine Dress Up
- Red Perrin Fender Shrouds
- Blue Torque Solutions Engine Pulley cover
- Blue Mishimoto Battery Tie Down
- Yellow Perrin Strut Tower Brace
- Red Process West Radiator Shroud

Most of my parts are from JDMuscle (@JDMuscleUSA on Instagram) and my wrap was done by The Lab North America (@TheLab.NA on Instagram). I'd highly recommend both companies. They're both amazing to work with.

In terms of future plans for the Subie, I'm not exactly sure. We'll see where the journey takes me.

Jonathan Golden
2005 Ferrari F430

Instagram: @lbwk430
Photographer: @merrick_media

I come from a car-loving family, my mom loves cars and got me into cars at a young age. She supported my love of cars and would take me out to the race tracks at a young age and then would even go with me to the illegal street races long before Fast and the Furious graced movie screens.

My wife is also an auto enthusiast but neither one of us is a purist, that's for sure. My wife and I actually met in the car scene. We've had a long, fun and sometimes stressful time with or over cars throughout our lives growing up and throughout the past fifteen years, we've been together.

We've owned and modified upwards of 30 different vehicles from Integra Type-R's, MR2's, FR-S, Mitsubishi's, tons of Nissan's from 240sx's, an RB26 powered Datsun 240z to an R35 GT-R, an Aston Martin Vantage, Mercedes E63 AMG rounded out with trucks and daily drivers as well as my wife's favourite of them all, her s197 Mustang.

I had seen and fell in love with the initial renderings and then press photos of the LibertyWalk kits Kato did on his 360 Modena and F430. Those images were embedded into my head and even though my wife and I most certainly weren't in a position to afford to purchase any model of Ferrari at the time, much less modify one, the images and ideas stuck. Those cars Kato built served as motivation.

-Thanks To-
- My wife Lisa
- My mom Linda
- Bobby & David at Sadistic Iron Werks
- Jason and Brian at Rotiform
- Stan at Toyo Tires
- Ryan at Accuair
- Art, Dave, Matt, Phillip and all the people at European Auto Group/GatedSix
- Merrick Harding at Merrick Media
- Toshi and Kato at Liberty Walk
- Diego at Low-Class Militia
- Tito Perez
- Maverick Sherrill
- Alfredo De Luna
- Joette Etchegoincelhay

In late 2016 during the annual SEMA crunch time I came across an Instagram post of an F430 getting fitted with a LibertyWalk kit here in the USA and began following the journey of that car knowing one day we'd have one.

We had decided in 2017 to start saving to get to a point to buy a 360 Modena and put some holes into it by installing a LibertyWalk kit. Flash forward to August of 2018 - a simple business trip with some fun stops mixed into it turned into a couple of hours at WekFest in downtown LA.

Cool cars, cool merch and one row of LibertyWalk grandiose nestled near the RWB collection. There was only one photo taken of that LBWK row, a picture my wife took of that very car I once saw an Instagram post of which would eventually be known as "The Red Car". Skip forward to December of that same year, suddenly

The Red Car had gone up for sale and so began a discussion about taking the plunge and if it was what we wanted to do as we already had another plan and also had never bought a car modified prior to purchase. We had always done our own modifications or had it done under our ownership, but this was a special situation.

It was The Red Car! Buying a supercar is a process, especially one so highly modified but we eventually got a deal worked out and it happened to sight unseen other than that day at WekFest LA and Instagram photos. The day came early January 2019 that the car was unloaded off of transport and wow, it was so surreal to have that car in our driveway.

We thought we'd get the car and just be able to enjoy the car without the processor money of going through building it from scratch. We were wrong. After receiving the car we quickly realized it was built to do one thing: look good sitting still.

We knew that was its main focus from the beginning, however the disregard of everything unseen when sitting still especially considering the reputation of the shop that built the car was appalling. Interior buttons didn't function, some were broken and held in with zip ties, interior and exterior panels were mostly loose and installed with mismatched hardware if any hardware at all, the exhaust was held in place with chain link fencing brackets, other exhaust flanges weren't tight, suspension and body components weren't tight and would cause horrible noises while driving, custom mounted Sparco seats hit the headliner,

tail light mounts glued together, body panels not aligned evenly, the fender cuts under the LibertyWalk kit were jagged, squared off and looked like they were attempted by a 5-year-old with safety scissors from elementary school resulting in deep tire cuts. The buyer's remorse hit strong, but there was only one thing to do.

Not having the time or means to really tackle all of this in our garage, I contacted the shop that had originally built the car. No real answers and the feeling that we weren't going to get anywhere unless we agreed to send the car and a blank check which based on what was sitting in our garage, didn't seem like a smart decision.

There weren't really any local shops that we felt confident could handle the enormous job of practically redoing the entire car so I began to look out of state and found Bobby at Sadistic Iron Werks in Hesperia California. After about two months of ownership, we loaded The Red Car on transport and off it went.

The plan was to completely redo the air suspension, build a full custom titanium exhaust, redo the LibertyWalk kit install and address all of the other problems. While Bobby had the car even more problems would be found behind the curtain of pretty paint and a big name shop build which just added more time before we could actually, hopefully, enjoy the car.

Months go by with the car getting worked on at Sadistic Iron Werks. New Crafted Suspension air struts and Accu air management had been installed, many issues were fixed and the car is now drive able! What now? You get the car wrapped green, wasabi green.

Swap out the ill-fitted Sparco's with Bride seats because what's better to pair with a JDM'dFerrari? Custom Rotiform wheels with Toyo tires and then it's time for SEMA with Accuair.

Finally driving the car, for what was really the first extended period of time around the Vegas strip under all of the lights was definitely making this journey more worth it! Post-SEMA saw the car back at Sadistic Iron Werks for a custom made chassis mount wing as well as finishing up the remainder of the probably long overdue maintenance.

So you've owned the car for two years and it's been gone about one year and nine months between all the new parts, fixing things and SEMA.
Any reasonable person would ship the car home to enjoy it. We're not those people. Off to San Antonio for a gated 6-speed manual conversion by European Auto Group.

It'll be more fun with the 3rd pedal and how can you not need a gated shifter in your F430!? This car may be beautiful, but it's still a drivers car and that's exactly what we're going to do - drive it. Hobbyists can't stop hobbying so we already have plans to reupholster the entire interior in black Alcantara and Rotiform is already working on a couple of new sets of wheels for the car.

Now if you asked me if we could go back in time and change anything, I'd tell you it would've been 100% cheaper, easier and less stressful to buy a stock F430 and build it up to this from scratch. However, I wouldn't change it as we've been able to meet so many great people and have such amazing experiences throughout this rocky road of a journey and truthfully make this car work the way it should've and is now so uniquely ours.

Exterior:
- Liberty Walk full F430 body kit
- Scuderia Style front bumper
- Scuderia Style rear bumper
- Scuderia rear grille
- Custom Chassis Mount wing
- Evasive Motorsports GTLM mirrors custom door mount

Interior:
- Bride Vorga seats
- Bride Seat brackets
- Gated Six-Speed Manual Conversion

Wheels/tires:
- Rotiform VDA
- F-20x9
- R-20x12
- Toyo T1R tires
- F- 245/30
- R- 315/25

Suspension:
- Crafted Suspension Company air struts with custom valving
- Accuair CVT
- Hardline Frunk design by Sadistic Iron Werks

Performance:
- Fabspeed headers
- Fabspeed carbon air boxes
- Fabspeed air filters
- Sadistic Iron Werks custom Titanium Test Pipes
- Sadistic Iron Werks custom Titanium rear exhaust section
- Tune

Armani Perez
2015 Honda Civic Si

Instagram: @rhdmani
Photographer: @fireblazinmedia

STANCEAUTOMAG PABLO COLON

My name is Armani Perez and I am from Miami Florida, but I'm currently living in Columbia, SC.

I'm fully immersed in the automotive industry in just about every aspect of my life, from my small detail business to my personal everyday life. I originally got interested in cars due to my uncle, he always was an automotive enthusiast.

He had everything from a Twin Turbo Dodge Stealth to a beautiful Evo X. We would sit up late at night when I was younger and play all the Need For Speed games and build the fastest and best-looking cars and the times we weren't playing the games I would watch him build and work on his own cars.

The older I got I knew I wanted to get into the same hobbies as him. I was the child who was always intrigued by cars and would try to memorize and name all the make and models that I would see on the road. I grew up in the early 2000s in Miami which arguably had one of the best car scenes in the world.

So as a kid I was heavily influenced by the cars I would see throughout the city of Miami.

My friends like Trevor North, Dalton Hale, and all the other great people I've met through social media have all had a huge impact on my wanting to keep building the car, as it makes for great conversations and memories along the way.

At the time of deciding what car I wanted to buy I really wasn't too sure of what platform I wanted to work on, but I definitely knew I wanted something modern but still very fun to drive. In the past, I owned a 1993 Nissan Skyline GTST 10th Anniversary Edition and two NB Miatas.

I knew the car had to be white and it had to have a 6-speed manual transmission. I've always been intrigued by Honda's and wondered why so many people hated these naturally aspirated 4 cylinders. I bought this used 2015 Honda Civic Si in June of 2020 and immediately started ordering parts. It got out of hand fast lol, but I've always wanted to build a car that I could drive every day and still look good and always be show-ready.

Out the gate, I knew I wanted to stance the car. I went ahead and ordered Air Lift 3p because in the past I was always static and for this build, I wanted the luxury of being able to drive low whenever I wanted and so I went straight to work on the car. I ended up going with a set of white GMR-04 Flow forged wheels for the simple fact that not a lot of people are running GMR wheels at the moment.

The car isn't the fastest, but it's very enjoyable for spirited driving especially when VTEC kicks in and it has the gas mileage to do it for weeks. I'm glad I went with a 9th Gen Si because to me it's the perfect daily driver while still maintaining all the aspects that make a car enjoyable to drive.

My plans for the car is to build a fun street car that I can enjoy and drive every day while keeping it reliable. I'm currently in the process to go full bolt-on and maybe turbo I'm the future.

I want to keep the car at a healthy 350-400hp which is more than enough for these lightweight cars. I plan on building the transmission to help with the torque and the power load that the car will put out. The car is currently being tuned by @yosh_tuned on Instagram which I highly recommend if you have any Honda platform.

All the suspension work was done by my friends at HNKS Performance who installed my Air Lift 3p and really helped me to see the vision for my car.

For the future of the car, I really want to wide-body the car with the "KevMannz Wide Body Kit" that he makes. I wanna follow that aggressive style of the wide body kit with the PRL Turbo kit which is the best and most popular kit in the market for these 9th Gens Civics.

I would love the wrap the car in a Sky Blue which I haven't seen before. This will help distinguish my car from the rest. To finally top off the build, I would want an aggressive set of Work Meister M1 3p to complement and finish the whole car.

At the end of the day when it comes down to it I'm really building this car to keep my mind in a positive place. Working on this car is my route to get away from all the negative things going on around the world and it really keeps me at peace doing so.

It gives me a huge sense of accomplishments to see this build through and to share the car with old friends as well as new friends

Exterior:
- Mugen Style Rain Visor
- 20% tint
- CaruseDesign Aero Flap
- Yellow tinted fog lights

Engine:
- Tsudo Catback exhaust
- CMT Racing Catless Down Pipe
- Hasport Motor Mounts
- AEM CAI

Wheels
- GMR-04 Flow Forged

Suspension
- Air Lift 3P
- Front camber plates
- Godspeed rear camber arms

Future Plans
- Widebody
- A wrap
- Turbo
- 3p Wheels

STANCEAUTOMAG PABLO COLON

Howard Carino

2017 Jeep Grand Cherokee Limited 3.6l V6

Instagram: @_biggiesmooth
Photographer: @jebkxymedia

I am from Delano, California and I am currently a full-time student going into my last semester of my bachelor's program at the California State University of Bakersfield. I am majoring in Liberal Studies and will be a Math Teacher in the future.

I am also an amateur barber and would like to attend barber school to obtain my barber's license. My barber page on Instagram is @biggiedabarber. I like to think that I am an advanced amateur barber with professional quality work.

I have always been into cars growing up. After watching the first Fast and the Furious movies, my love for JDM cars especially grew. Paul Walker became a hero to me and someone I looked up to.

Naturally, the Nissan Skyline GTR R34 became my ultimate dream car and still is. I hope to one day own an R34, a JDM Legend. This is the first car that I bought and the first car that I have ever worked on.

I have always had an admiration for SUVs because they look beefy and aggressive. The Jeep Grand Cherokees had always caught my eye especially because of the big, aggressive and sporty look. Also, it's perfect for long drives because of the comfort of the car and the modern Technology put into it.

Driving my car is so relaxing and joyful. Driving a car that I have worked on gives me so much pride and when someone compliments my car, I get so happy. I found that working on my car and spending time with it is my outlet in life, my escape from my stressful school life.

Advice/Tips

This car is so versatile. There are so many ways you could take this car with the build. The more common way is an off-road build and there are so many parts online to help you out with this type of build.

But there is also the street build where it's more sporty and more focused on lowering the car instead of lifting it. It may seem like it yet, but I am going for more of a JDM inspired build.

If you are trying to go for the same look as me, I suggest buying the right body parts first and then focus on paint or wrap. Also, buy the right offset for the wheels. The lower the offset the better because it will look way more aggressive.

What makes it Unique?

My car is a Jeep Grand Cherokee that is not lifted or a 4x4. I think that's the first thing people will think once they see my car because most Jeeps are off-road builds but looking at my car with the orange colour shift wrap makes it stand out.

Also the way I plan to build this car, not many have done with this car specifically. I plan to lower it eventually on air bag suspension.

Groups/Clubs

I was a founding member of a car group based in Delano, California. I am the Person In Charge, P.I.C., for Invictus. Our Instagram is @invictus__hq.

The car scene/club has helped me with knowledge of cars. How to work on them to know the engine of every car. They have just given me a lot of information regarding JDM cars and cars in general.

I installed the headlights as well as the tint overlays of the car. I took apart the exterior and deleted most of the chrome of the car.

Future Plans
I plan to convert the whole body into an SRT body and I plan to put the car on air bag suspension. I want to paint the car, Nardo Grey.

Spec List

- Anzo Headlights
- Cruxmoto tail light overlays
- Full car wrap
- Titanium Burnt exhaust tips
- Full Chrome delete
- Srt Hellcat Replica Rims
- Painted my engine bay red
- Resonator Delete
- Muffler delete
- Iron man Racing Tires

STANCEAUTOMAG JARED KIBLER

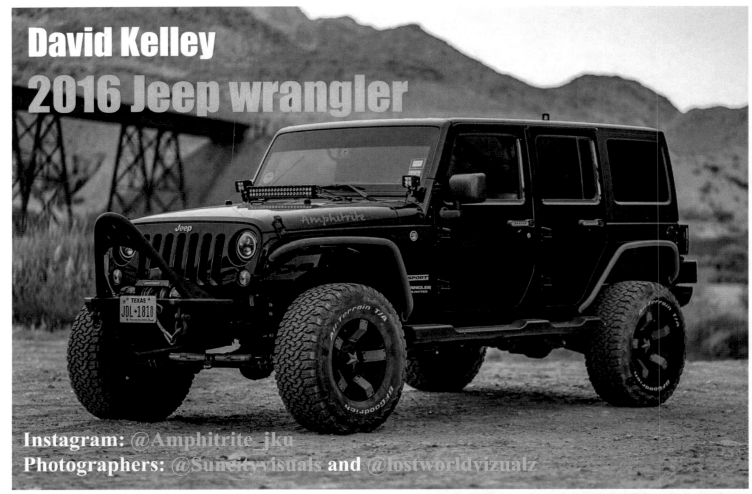

David Kelley
2016 Jeep wrangler

Instagram: @Amphitrite_jku
Photographers: @Suncityvisuals and @lostworldvizualz

I am originally from El Paso; however, I am going to school in Dallas, Texas. Currently, I am a college student studying computer science. Currently, I am planning on graduating next spring, and plan on starting a career in the computer security industry. I have been in love with cars pretty much my entire life, and spend most of my free time going to car shows or building my car (as well as friend's cars).

This may sound a little corny, but my main interest in cars started when I originally watched the original Fast and Furious. Just watching the build process on those cars just intrigued me, and made me realize that building cars was a hobby for me.

My passion for cars really grew this past year when I joined my first car club(@simplysinful_elpaso). This team allowed me to be a part of something a little bit bigger in the car scene.

When I was seventeen, my parents bought this Jeep for me, and the build process began soon after that. I have worked every day since then to be able to afford the parts that are on there now. This car let my childhood fantasy come to life, and I finally had a chance to build my own car.

Why this Vehicle?

In El Paso, the off-road community was very large, and the idea of being able to drive through the sand dunes really intrigued me.

On top of this, I had seen the after market support for Jeeps, as well as how easy they were to modify. All of these factors contributed to my love for Jeeps, and to this day I would not have done anything differently.

Driving a modified car is the best feeling ever. During the summers, you can take the top and doors off, and just let the air rush through your hair.

When you're at shows there are many little Jeep things you can do like "flex" off other Jeeps, that really just draw a crowd. When people walk up to me it really is an eye-opening experience. It's an amazing feeling when someone likes your build so much they want to know what parts you have.

What makes it unique?

One thing that I think makes the Jeep stand out is the combination of parts. Most Jeep owners usually stick to one brand when it comes to fenders, bumpers, and armour. I purposely chose to use different brands for the fenders and the bumpers.

This gives me some variation that some people don't have. On top of this, I have only seen one Jeep to this day that has the same paint job and colours that I have. Within the next month, the Jeep will be even more unique once I get it wrapped.

Advice/Tips

One of the biggest tips I can give for someone considering buying a Jeep is doing lots of research. There are a lot of brands, and different nuances, that give you many options.

There are tons of Facebook/ Reddit groups that are dedicated to everything Jeep; some even in your area. These groups can give you valuable information, as well as give you an opportunity to make new friends.

Jeeps are extremely easy to modify. Between the ground clearance, which makes it easy to crawl under, and the ample room in the engine bay, Jeeps, in my opinion, are extremely easy to make your own.

One tip I would give is to watch videos of someone installing the same parts. Some bolts are hard to find, and these videos, most of the time, show you every little detail that the instructions don't.

Spec List

Engine:
- K&N intake
- Throttle body spacer

Suspension:
- 4" Rancho lift

Wheels/Tires:
- 35" BF Goodrich tires
- 17" XD Rockstar 2 wheels

Lighting:
- Sunpie RGB headlights
- KC light bars and rock lights

Body:
- Poison Spyder crusher fenders
- DV8 inner fender liners
- Smittybilt XRC bumpers

Exhaust:
- Flow master outlaw axle back

Misc:
- Dual battery kit
- Teraflex sway bar quick disconnects
- JL 12" subwoofers x2

Everything except for the lift and wheels/ tires has been done by me. The company that installed the lift was a local El Paso company named 4wheelcenter.

Future Plans
The next thing that is being done is a wrap installed by @sinfulwraps915. After the wrap, the next mod going to be done is a 392 swap. Once this is done, I plan on doing many modifications, such as a supercharger, headers, cams, tune, etc.

Groups/Clubs
Currently, I am a member of two clubs. My main club is @simplysinful_elpaso. This group is basically family, and I spend every minute of my time in El Paso with them. The other club I'm a part of is North Texas Jeep Club. This is my main off-roading club.

The car scene has done several things. The one that was most impactful for me has been giving me a new family, as well as many new friends. On top of this, I have also gotten a few sponsors that are helping me build the Jeep even more.

Jesse Perez,
2003 AWD Chevy Silverado SS

Instagram: @Sinister_SS_0
Photographer: @oadam7
Facebook: @SinisterSS03
Youtube: jay35088

I am 28, from Corpus Christi, TX. I am an automotive technician. I've always liked to tinker and mess with cars but when the first fast and the furious movie came out it just opened my eyes to so much more possibilities.

Going from messing with cars to pass time to making it a lifestyle and finding a group of friends that grow into family and help each other with their builds. Pretty much sums up where I am today. I've always been a Chevy guy whether it be cars or trucks.

Don't get me wrong I love imports and all kinds of other builds too, but trucks suit me better for a few reasons!

My current project/daily is a 2003 AWD Chevy Silverado SS aka "Sinister SS". It was always a dream of mine to one day find a clean unmolested SS, I could modify and put my own personal touches on.

One of the big reasons I have always wanted one of these trucks is because of their smooth, yet aggressive body lines, plus the fact that the first few years these trucks were produced were AWD, which surprisingly, not a lot of people knew.

For me it's just a big wow factor, not many people expect a full-size truck to ever be AWD from the factory and that's what makes this truck so unique and a great platform to begin building on.

This build started when I was browsing the Facebook marketplace, and I came across an ad for a 2003 Silverado SS from a local Chevy dealership I used to work at.

After browsing the ad it seemed a bit suspicious for being too clean of a truck for the year and mileage.

I called my buddy, John Aldrich that worked there, for his opinion on the condition of the truck. After talking to him and hearing what other people were saying I got the impression this was a very solid truck. I got the keys from him and test drove the truck. I immediately fell in love and felt right at home behind the wheel.

The only issue was that another customer had made an appointment to test drive the truck and do a credit application to potentially purchase the truck. I slowly began to feel like this truck was slipping away before I even owned it.

I gave my contact info to a salesman at the dealership and told him to call me if for some reason the customer did not show up or did not like the truck. I walked out with very low expectations of getting a call back at all.

I told myself "if it's meant to be, everything will just fall into place" The next day I got a call from that salesman saying the customer did not show and if I still wanted the truck, I should get my ass down there as quickly as possible since there was a high possibility the truck was going to be sent to an auto auction.

I got down to the dealership to close and sign on the truck shortly after getting off the phone with the salesman.

Fast forward a few weeks later, I got a call from the same salesman that had helped me get the truck. He informed me that the previous owner of the SS was there and would like to talk to me. I ended up meeting the previous owner that same day. I gave him the address of the shop I was currently working at.

He got out and pulled out a big box from his back seat of his brand new 2019 Chevy Silverado RST. Inside the box were a bunch of brand-new parts he had that he never got to install.

Also inside the box was a thick folder that contained the original window sticker, documentation, and service records on the truck dating back to the day it rolled off the dealership lot back in early 2003. At that point, I knew I hit the jackpot and bought the perfect truck.

I was the 2nd and proud owner of a properly documented and maintained AWD Silverado SS.

Since the truck was entirely bone stock it was a great platform to build on, I did not have to worry about trying to fix anyone else's mistakes. This truck came factory with a pretty stout drive train, which included a 6.0L LQ9 that was begging for some performance parts.

Engine/Transmission Performance mods
- Speed engineering 1 7/8 long tube header
- Speed engineering cat-less y pip
- Borla XR1 exhaus
- Trailblazer SS intake manifold swap with bigger 50l injectors
- Ported and polished LS3 throttle body with x lin harness
- MSD 2 step/launch controlle
- OEM electric fan conversion with Nelson performanc harness
- Cold air intak
- Transgo HD2 shift kit with Sonnex billet super hol servo
- Tru cool 40k trans cooler with Glenn's aut performance bracket kit
- Custom Volatile Performance 93 octane street tun

Cosmetic Modifications
- Steel 2-inch cowl induction ho
- Custom designed racing stripes cut and laid by T Sheets of @ghostcustomsgraphics
- Led tail lights with matching led third brake lig
- Custom moulded 3-piece wing   @mandospaint
- Custom painted front bowtie (blackou
- Custom painted grille and bumper mesh (blackou

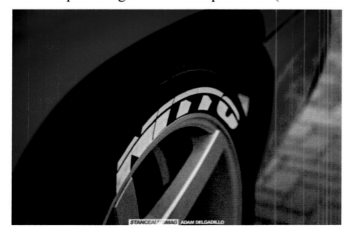

Interior modifications
- Custom upholstered red & pewter leather seats wit custom red SS logo embroidered in the front and rear of the headrest
- Kenwood double din touch screen radio with backu camera custom mounted in tailgate handle bezel
- Custom ported under-seat box with 4 8" skar audi VD8D2 subs
- DS18 pro audio 6.5" mid-range speakers front an rear with 2" DS18 super bullet tweeters in front doors

Wheels, Tires & suspension
- 22x9.5 6x5.5 +24mm offset machined face with silv barrel Strada Perfetto wheels (special thanks to Rico over @Stradawheels for hooking me up with these wheels)
- 275/40R22 white letter Nitto 420V tir
- 2/4 drop kit which includes 2-inch front dr spindles, 2-inch drop shackles and 2-inch drop hangers for the rear along with belltech street performance drop shocks

As far as future plans go, just shortly after Adam Delgadillo worked his magic behind the camera Lens I ordered a Texas speed cam kit and Circle D 3200 stall converter, which hopefully by the end of April these parts will be installed in the truck along with a new set of 243 cylinder heads.

I will then be, close to or exactly where I want to be for this truck. I will continue to daily drive the truck while still being able to take it to the drag strip on the weekends!

Andreas Tatt
Ford Focus ST 2014
Photographer: @lyonsautomotive

I'm 30 years old and I'm based in Canterbury, Kent. After graduating from University in Bristol, I managed to find a job in open cast mining in Western Australia. What was meant to be 6/12 months of "real-world experience" turned into a 5-year stay in Perth.

A change in circumstances meant I headed back home to the UK to go into the family business which publishes Greetings Cards. My hobbies include tinkering with my car, smoking meat and to keep fit, I play a lot of badminton.

My dad got me into cars. We watched Top Gear a lot and other motoring shows. In Perth, once I'd built up enough money, the first thing on my mind was to buy a car. I'd previously had an MK3 Focus in England which I really liked but wished it had more power, therefore the MK3 Focus ST was the car for me.

I found an ST owners club on Facebook - WA 5 Pots and EcoBooST4's and quickly made some great friends. Soon the mod bug bit me - most likely from fellow ST friends in the area. Going to the few cars shows there are in Perth spurred me on to develop my car and make it my own.

My MK3 ST is my 5th car but my first "performance" car and certainly the first car I've modded. I started off with an S reg Fiat Punto, then a Corsa before moving to Fords - MK7 Fiesta and MK3 Focus Titanium.

The ST was the perfect car for me. Best "bang for the buck," I think. It's easily modified, cheap to run and fun to drive. When I was looking for a car, I quickly narrowed my options down to two - a Golf GTi and the Focus ST.

I looked at the Golf first. I was quickly put off by the salesman who was trying to sway/bully me into buying a car there and then. His attempt to impress me by speeding down back roads was not working.

The car itself was impressive but without extras was already more expensive than the ST. To me, although the GTi was a good car, it didn't put a smile on my face. The ST on the other hand was cheaper, better looking in my eyes, more fun to drive and most importantly, had me smiling all through the test drive.

I absolutely love my ST. It's very cliché, but like a lot of car fanatics, I can't help but turn and look at it when I walk away. I've made it my own and it makes me feel really good that others really like it too! I never set out to have the fastest/most modified ST in the car scene but something that would turn a few heads.

My ST is now quite distinctive and I often have people ask me at shows whether this is the Australian ST?

Early on, I decided to purchase a Quaife LSD in Mountune's Christmas sales. If you can, whilst installing the LSD, upgrade your clutch too. It'll be the same amount of labour whether you do the clutch at the same time or not, so effectively the labour for the clutch would be free.

At the time, the only after market clutches available for the MK3 ST were for bigger power 400hp+ from the US - something I didn't need, nor had the money for.

The obvious "feature" of my ST is the wrap. It's 3M's Satin Flip Volcanic Flare. I loved the flake in the OEM Tangerine Scream but I wanted to stand out from the crowd a bit. It's not the kind of wrap I'd recommend to everyone though - stain effect wraps easily mark and attract dust. It's not a finish I'd recommend for a daily driver for sure!

Future Plans

There are a couple of mods in mind - potentially world firsts but they're rather tricky so are taking some time. I don't drive the car enough (weekend car) to warrant going big turbo so for now, I think I'm at a stage where I can enjoy the car.

Tips/Advice

My advice would be, start with a stock car if you can. The enjoyment of working on this car has been mainly due to learning as much as I can about how it works and how it's put together.

To fully appreciate modding it, start from scratch, do a LOT of research and ask as many questions as you can - no matter how silly you think they are!

Also, find a great mechanic, preferably someone who actually cares for customers cars and understands your wants/needs. In Australia, a good friend of mine, who is a professional mechanic, set up his own business - Perth Performance Parts, which I regularly took my ST to for adding parts and servicing.

In the UK, I found BRC Performance who are fairly local to me. They specialise in Fast Fords so know these cars like the back of their hand which puts my mind at ease. This tip is well known throughout the car scene but when I came to do it, I had very few options.

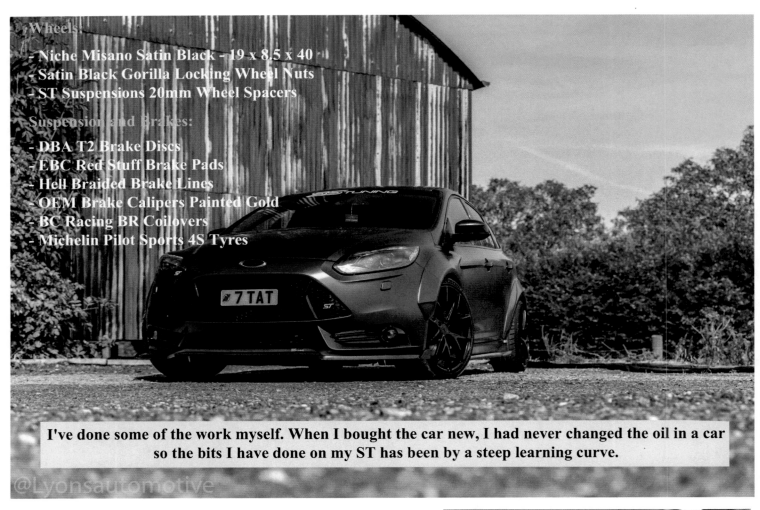

Wheels:
- Niche Misano Satin Black - 19 x 8.5 x 40
- Satin Black Gorilla Locking Wheel Nuts
- ST Suspensions 20mm Wheel Spacers

Suspension and Brakes:
- DBA T2 Brake Discs
- EBC Red Stuff Brake Pads
- Hell Braided Brake Lines
- OEM Brake Calipers Painted Gold
- BC Racing BR Coilovers
- Michelin Pilot Sports 4S Tyres

I've done some of the work myself. When I bought the car new, I had never changed the oil in a car so the bits I have done on my ST has been by a steep learning curve.

@Lyonsautomotive

Exterior:

- Wrapped in 3M Satin Flip Volcanic Flare
- Custom Headlights by Monkey Wrench Bespoke
- Custom Light Up ST Grille Logo by Monkey Wrench Bespoke
- Gel Badges by Gel Badges Australia
- Body Kit by SS-Tuning
- Front Splitter,
- Side Skirts,
- 20mm Fender Flares,
- Rear Diffuser
- Delta Styling S-RR Spoiler (Double Carbon Fibre Blades)
- Kaylan Mud flaps - Performance Creations UK
- Shark Fin Aerial - Visual Garage

Interior:

- SS-Tuning Carbon Fibre Steering Wheel,
- Carbon Fibre Handbrake,
- Carbon Fibre Gear Knob
- Custom NJ Devils Gauge Background Plates
- Pioneer MVH-Z5050BT Head Unit with AERPRO Fascia

Protection:

- Wrap Ceramic Coated with Kamikaze Collection's Film Surface Coat
- Wheels Ceramic Coated with Kamikaze Collection's Stance Rim Coat
- Glass Ceramic Coated with Kamikaze Collection's Intenso Window Coat

Engine:
- Cobb Accessport - Stratified Tuned
- Cobb Intercooler + Hard Pipes
- Cobb Rear Motor Mount
- Turbosmart Recalculation Valve
- Custom Performance Engineering
- Cold Air Intake in Tangerine Scream
- PumaSpeed Short Shift Swing Arm
- Boomba Racing Shifter Bushings
- Boomba Racing Intake Manifold and Throttle Body Spacers
- Mishimoto Coolant Tank
- Tangerine Scream Silicone Hoses - Pro Hoses
- Carbon Fibre Skinned Battery Cover and Fuse Cover
- Majestic Performance Oil Catch Can
- NB Styling Bonnet Struts
- Velossa Tech Big Mouth
- Dark Ice Designs Engine Dress Up Kit
- Custom Turbo-Back 3" Exhaust to 4" Tips
- Cobb Exhaust Hangers
- Quaife Limited Slip Differential

Groups/Clubs
I'm part of various Facebook groups some as an admin/
moderator role and others as an enthusiast.
Some of my favourite groups include:
- MK3 ST/RS Owners UK
- Ford Mania UK
- Shadow Car Culture
The group that started my relationship with the car community -
WA 5 Pots and EcoBoost 4s

Being in a Community, I've made some great friends in these
groups and love to pass on experiences/advice I've picked up
over the years from working on my ST. I like to see what others
are doing with their cars.

Not everything is to my taste but I can appreciate the hard work
and passion that might have gone into that modification. Being
able to pass on things I've learnt from working on my car to
others is something I enjoy. Giving recommendations, helping
others and seeing creations come to life is a great feeling.

Shout Outs
- Exhaust - Custom Exhaust Specialists - Perth, Western Australia
- General Mechanics - Perth Performance Parts - Perth, Western Australia
- Gel Badges - Gel Badges Australia - Perth, Western Australia
- Servicing/MOT/Parts Fitting - BRC Performance - Ashford, Kent
- Wrap supplied by Bosho Industries - Perth, Western Australia
- Wrap Installed by Jon Quantico - Perth, Western Australia
- Custom Headlights - Monkey Wrench Bespoke - Chesterfield, Derbyshire
- Detailing - Alchemy Automotive Detailing - Perth, Western Australia

Made in the USA
Middletown, DE
21 November 2022

15647124R00029